PEMBREY COPPERWORKS SCHOOL
IN VICTORIAN TIMES

Graham Davies

Ellen Davies

First published in 2021 by Pembrey and Burry Port Heritage Group

Second Edition 2022

© **Graham Davies, Ellen Davies**

Every effort has been made to contact copyright holders of photographs. However, the authors will rectify in future editions any inadvertent omissions brought to their attention.

All rights reserved. No part of this publication may be reproduced, stored in a retrieval system, or transmitted, in any form or by any means without the prior permission of the publishers.

Cover design by Alan Williams

ALL PROCEEDS FROM THE SALE OF THIS BOOK GO TO PEMBREY AND BURRY PORT HERITAGE GROUP

EARLY EDUCATION IN WALES

In the 18th century it was religion and charity that promoted most of the education in Wales. Church organisations and charitable institutions, along with a large number of private schools, were the main providers. The Sunday schools were very popular since they used the Welsh language, reflected the Welsh nonconformist beliefs and traditions, were available free of charge to all ages and did not interfere with everyday work.

Griffith Jones' Circulating Schools

Griffiths Jones was born in Carmarthenshire in 1683 and he conceived the idea of a 'circulating school' for the rural parishes where a school building was not feasible. He suggested money should be spent on teachers who would hold classes for three months in a parish vestry or other available building and in that way reach out to large numbers of people with the least expense. The teaching was in Welsh and the focus

Griffiths Jones
Wikimedia Commons

was on reading the Bible and the Catechism. His schools are regarded as instrumental in making Wales a literate nation and their fame spread throughout Europe.

Thomas Charles and the Sunday School Movement

Courtesy
Wikimedia Commons

Born near St. Clears in 1755, Charles was a Methodist leader and popular preacher in north Wales. He continued to advance the circulating school with up to seven teachers paid for by collections made in Methodist Societies. However, he is best known for the development of the Sunday School movement, building on the work of Robert Raikes but continuing the adult classes and using the Welsh language. The movement grew rapidly with the aim of learning reading through the Bible, so that 'souls could be saved', and learning the catechism by rote.

The Society for the Promotion of Christian Knowledge (SPCK) was formed in 1699 by a group of friends, among whom was the industrialist Sir Humphrey Mackworth of Neath. They were concerned about the "growth of vice and immorality" and 'ignorance of the Christian religion' in the country and raised funds for schools for the poor across England and Wales. Their aim was to enable people to read the Bible, live morally and be useful in society. Some regarded this as social conditioning to ensure that the 'lower orders' realised their position in society.

The established church had always regarded itself as the main provider of education and the Anglican-based school system was often resisted in nonconformist Wales. So initially the Church was hostile to the work of the Quaker **Joseph Lancaster**. He set up in 1801 an elementary school for poor children in London and devised a 'monitorial system' using older students to teach the younger ones. It avoided the payment of additional teachers and enabled free education of a large number of children. One 'schoolmaster' might be responsible for up to 300 children in one large schoolroom.

Joseph Lancaster
Courtesy Wikimedia Commons

The British and Foreign Schools Society

Lancaster's initiative led in 1814 to the founding of the **British and Foreign Schools Society** (BFSS) in London. It established a number of what were called 'British Schools' (as opposed to 'National Schools') and teacher training institutions and also provided funding for books and equipment. It was from the 1840s onwards that it began to have an impact in Wales.

The National Society

This was the Anglican response to the founding of the BFSS and aimed to set up a National School in each parish in opposition to the British Schools which were non-denominational. Children would be taught the 3Rs, to read the Bible, to learn the basics of the Scriptures and the Catechism and be provided with adequate books. Despite their advantage in funding, by 1846 of the 1100 church schools in Wales only 377 were linked to the National Society.

The 'Treason of the Blue Books'

In 1847 a report into the state of education in Wales was published by the British government following an inspection of schools by a team of commissioners. The report came to be known as the 'Treason of the Blue Books' from the colour of its cover, and because it caused a furore especially with regard to derogatory comments made about the behaviour and morals of the Welsh people.

Depiction of the Rebecca Riots
Courtesy Wikimedia Commons

No doubt the rioting in Merthyr, the Rebecca Riots and the Chartist uprising in Newport presented a picture of discontent. Certainly industrialisation resulted in appalling living and working conditions, poverty and unrest. For many the cause was the lack of adequate education and the predominance of the Welsh language which was believed to be holding the back the Welsh worker.

The report was scathing in its attack on the state of education in Wales; the tone was often derisory and the approach lacking in empathy. It portrayed an insufficient number of schools, inadequately trained teachers and too few children attending school and with irregular attendance. The reason for the latter was often the inability to pay the school pence and family responsibilities. The teaching of English, the medium of instruction in most schools, was poor and some teachers had little knowledge of the language. Others used English text books which the children could not read.

In truth, the educational situation was extremely poor, but no poorer than many areas in England. The commissioners in fact recognised the hunger that the Welsh had for education and praised the work of the Sunday Schools. What the grim report did was to harden attitudes toward Anglicanism, increase the support for Nonconformism and galvanise the societies responsible for the provision of education in Wales.

Robert Raikes, pioneer of the Sunday School Movement
Courtesy Wikimedia Commons

This, then, was the background to the development of works schools in Wales and the 'Blue Books' report was published in the decade before the building of the Copperworks School in Burry Port.

THE GROWTH OF 'WORKS SCHOOLS' IN SOUTH WALES

With the growth of a variety of industries in the 19th century – mining, iron smelting, copper smelting, tinplate – came the growth of population from the workers in the townships that sprang up. This raised issues of housing, sanitation and education. There had been grammar schools for the affluent from the 16th century but the lack of state education meant that up until the second half of the 19th century in Wales education was provided by National and British Schools, private schools, Sunday Schools and works schools. Generally, the state of education in Wales was grim, a 'destitution' shared also by housing and sanitation.

Copper works in Swansea
Courtesy Wikimedia Commons

It was factory legislation that not only gradually improved conditions but also facilitated education for those children and young people in their industries. However, the legislation did not apply to Wales and although the proprietors of works were not obliged to provide schools, many of them did. At first there was opposition: from those who favoured the Sunday Schools since they were free, all age and did not conflict with the weekly work, and also from those who did not regard schooling as necessary for their employment. However, generally the people of Wales were enthusiastic about receiving an education.

Other issues affected progress in the development of education in Wales. One was the issue of the *Welsh language* since, although teaching in the Sunday Schools was in Welsh, lessons in the day schools were in English. This applied to the works schools and particularly with the owners, proprietors and officials predominantly English speaking. The second issue was *religion*. Certainly the government had viewed education as philanthropic and the responsibility of voluntary societies and works proprietors, and many people resisted state intervention seeing the move as secularization in the education system. Yet the main problem had always been resentment of the Nonconformists towards any attempt to impose an Anglican system.

In the middle of the 19th century there was a marked increase in the number of works schools and these needed to affiliate to one of the two voluntary societies in order to qualify for a government grant for buildings, salaries and equipment. Both the Llanelli and Pembrey Copperworks schools aligned themselves with the British and Foreign Schools Society which was non-denominational and would have appealed to the predominantly nonconformist working classes. In such schools the men were happier to pay the obligatory school pence.

Probably the first works school in South Wales was established in Neath in 1705 by Sir Humphrey Mackworth for 40 children of his mine workers. But most were set up in the beginning of the 19th century by the owners of the copper smelting works. The largest and most successful were built by the Vivians of Swansea and the Nevills of Llanelli.

The first Swansea works schools, the Kilvey Copperworks Schools at Foxhole, were linked to **the White Rock copper companies** and their proprietors Grenfell and Freeman. The schools, for girls, boys and infants, opened in 1806 and were maintained by a stoppage of 1d from the workmen. Grenfell says that he visited the infant school and heard a 'gallery lesson': there was a stand with a frame into which scriptural prints were placed and discussed.

Copyright unknown

The Hafod copperworks schools were built in 1847 by the Vivian family who were deeply aware of the lack of educational facilities in the Swansea district. They saw education as essential for industrial efficiency and the schools were regarded as outstanding examples of their type. They were run efficiently with fully trained teachers assisted by pupil-teachers, and based on child-centred Pestalozzian principles – 'head, hands and heart'.

In Llanelli the school built by the **Nevills,** developed from a free school originally in the yard of the Copperworks, opened in 1846 for boys and infants with the girls' school following in 1852. It served the employees of the many industrial companies of the Nevills, but also admitting other children. It was financed by stoppages and school pence. Regarded as one of the best in Wales, the curriculum also included scientific and technical subjects and offered a variety of evening classes.

Opened in 1855, the Pembrey Copperworks School consisted of two schoolrooms, for boys and girls, each 62 x 20 ft. and one for infants , 30 x 24 ft. The building cost £1,700 and the fees initially were: for boys and girls of the Works' employees, 1½d each week deducted from the workmen's wages; for other children, 2d. This raised around £90 each year, whereas the expenditure was about £200. The deficiency was covered by the proprietors of the Copper Works as was also the cost of slates and books. By 1868 the fees had risen to 2d and 3d and the majority of pupils at the school were 'outside' children – 265 as opposed to 214 workmen's children.

The school displayed some of the man characteristics of the works school including an infant school and an extended curriculum compared to the other day schools. The larger works schools offered a more advanced curriculum akin to the German schools of the day. Llanelli Copperworks School, for example, taught land surveying, algebra, geometry, astronomy and practical and inorganic chemistry for older boys. In Pembrey the curriculum was taught through the medium of English and focused on the '3 Rs'. In addition, the girls were taught scripture, geography, sewing, cutting out, knitting and domestic economy, and the boys scripture, history, vocal music and mapping.

Works schools generally provided a superior education to the day schools, were able to pay teachers a higher salary and many offered apprentices' day classes and evening schools. At the time when use of the monitorial system was decreasing and more teachers were being employed Pembrey School used the popular pupil-teacher strategy while still retaining monitors. Most of the works schools affiliated to one of the two voluntary societies through which the government gave grants for employing teachers and training pupil-teachers. Many benefited both from the grants and the 'poundage' collected from the employees. In fact Pembrey was able to receive poundage and fees from external pupils (school pence).

Pembrey Copperworks School   *Copyright Ray Hobbs*

PEMBREY COPPERWORKS SCHOOL – THE EARLY DAYS

The Copper Works at Pembrey was built in 1849 by Messrs. Mason and Elkington, who came from Birmingham and London respectively. The **Copperworks School** was opened in August 1855 as three schools – girls, infants and boys. Built for the workers employed by Mason and Elkington in their copper works, collieries, and brickworks, the buildings cost £1,700 of which the entire sum was contributed by the Company, with £270 for its upkeep.

Josiah Mason
Courtesy Josiah Mason

George Elkington
Wikimedia Commons

Works schools needed to affiliate to one of the two voluntary societies in order to obtain a government grant. Pembrey was linked to the British and Foreign Schools Society which mainly reflected the nonconformity in Wales. The other society was the National Society linked to the Anglican church. However, the proprietors agreed to the establishment of a non-denominational or non-sectarian school in which the Bible was the sole basis for religious instruction, no church catechism was used and children of any religious background or creed were admitted.

Another important feature was that no preference was given to children who had been educated in the copperworks school when vacancies arose at the works. The main criteria were ability and skill. Ten years following the opening the majority of pupils at the school were 'outside' children, whose parents were not employed at the works.

In 1858 the head teachers of the girls' and infants' and of the boys' school completed questionnaires for the British and Foreign School Society. Copies, which were obtained from their archives, provide information for the first two years of the schools. The boys' school Head was Richard Williams and the girls' and infants' school Head was Sarah Furnaess or Furness.

THE BOYS' SCHOOL questionnaire was signed by head teacher Richard Williams and dated December 17, 1858. Information is given for the years 1856 and 1857. The official name of the school was Pembrey Copper Works School and it was intended to accommodate 150 children. The head teacher describes the area as a mix of agricultural, mining and manufacturing. The total number of scholars belonging to the school was about 120. There was no evening school provided at that time. The staffing comprised one paid master, two pupil-teachers and one monitor.

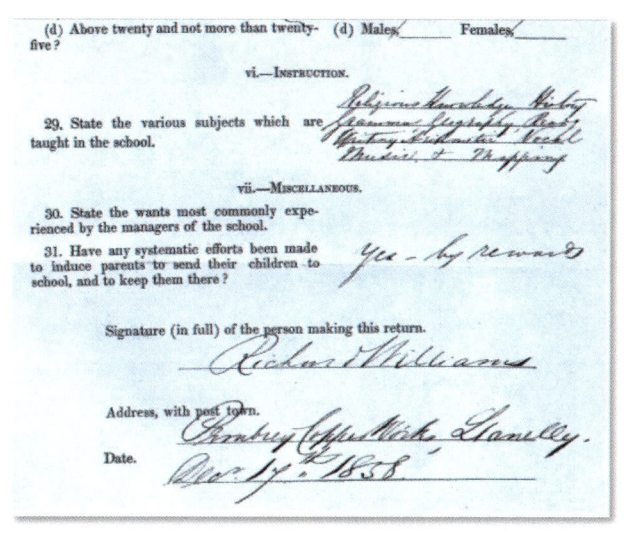

Courtesy British & Foreign School Society

On the day of the return the following numbers of boys were in attendance: above six years of age and not more than nine - 29 boys; above nine and not more than twelve - 27 boys; above twelve years and not more than thirteen - 16 boys; above 13 years and not more than fifteen - 4 boys; above fifteen years and not more than twenty -3 boys.

The average age at which the boys were admitted into the school was nine years and the average age at which they left the school was 11 years and decreasing.

The subjects taught in the school were religious knowledge, history, grammar, geography, reading, writing, arithmetic, vocal music and mapping.

THE GIRLS' SCHOOL return was signed by the headmistress Sarah Furnaess on December 17, 1858. The school catered for infant boys and girls of all ages. At the time of the questionnaire there were 34 infant boys and 148 girls belonging to the school. There was no evening school at that time. Staffing comprised one paid mistress and one assistant mistress, two pupil teachers and three monitors.

On the day on which the return was made the following numbers of girls and infant boys were in attendance: under three years of age - 6 boys and 4 girls; from three to six years of age - 11 boys, 14 girls; above six years of age and not more than nine - 29 girls; above nine years of age and not more than twelve - 32 girls; above twelve years of age and not more than 13 - 9 girls; above thirteen years of age and not more than fifteen - 10 girls; above fifteen years of age and not more than twenty - 3 girls. The average age at which girls leave the school was 13 and decreasing.

Courtesy British & Foreign School Society

In 1856 the total number of scholars 'belonging' to the school was 13 boys, and 134 girls. In 1857 the number was 21 boys and 152 girls. In 1857 the total number of scholars who attended the school during 176 whole days was 2 infant boys and 47 girls.

The subjects taught at the school were Scripture, reading, writing, arithmetic, grammar, geography, sewing, cutting out, knitting, domestic economy.

THE OPENING OF THE SCHOOL 22nd August 1855

There are two newspaper accounts of the opening. In **'Y Diwygiwr'** local minister Rev. Henry Evans describes the building as splendid, beautifully painted with colourful maps hanging on the walls. A lot of the company's employees and their wives were present and up to 500 people enjoyed tea and cakes provided by the company. Mr Apsley Smith of New Lodge in his speech encouraged the parents to support the headteachers, to show interest in their children's work and to keep the children clean. He also made clear the distinction between the non-denominational Copperworks School and others in the area supported by the National Society.

In the 'Welshman' the reporter describes the building as very 'capacious', consisting of boys' and girls' schoolrooms, and two class rooms. The schoolrooms ran parallel to each other and were 63 feet by 24 feet and about 14 feet high. "On entering the boys' school the visitors were struck with the very elegant appearances of the decorations and festoons of flowers and evergreens were dispersed with great profusion and taste. Maps and illustrations from scripture, natural philosophy and the mechanical powers were there in abundance and, as a crowning piece, there was a beautiful device of flowers and evergreens with the initial letters 'M' and 'E' (Mason and Elkington) …" There seemed to be lots of books of every kind and the building also included a public library and reading room.

The report in the *Welshman* went on to praise the employees – "During the evening the order and decorum of this large concourse of workmen and their families did not fail to convince every visitor that Messrs. Mason and Elkington were favoured with steady and industrious employees". The ladies "who served the tea with untiring zeal" were thanked and each one named. Also mentioned were the 'great and the good' of Pembrey and Burry Port who were in attendance, with some well-known family names recorded: for example, McKiernon, Wedge, Parkes, Stanley.

Interestingly, the names absent in both accounts are those of the headteachers, an indication of the fairly lowly status of teachers at this time. The meeting ended with three cheers to be given to Messrs. Mason and Elkington "for the handsome manner in which they had been entertained, which was responded to with enthusiasm".

LIFE IN A 19th CENTURY WORKS SCHOOL

The Pembrey Copperworks School developed a good reputation as HMI reports bear witness: For example, *"This school is in excellent order",* 1868; *"This school is in very good order"* – 1870.

The school day began after what was for most children a long trudge to school in often cold, wet weather. At 9 o'clock the **school bell** signaled a military style line up and march into assembly for prayers, religious instruction and any announcements. Boys and girls were at first taught in one building but in separate schools divided by a wooden partition, with infants a part of the girls' school.

Both schools were initially divided by age into six standards, but if children didn't reach the appropriate level they would stay down and repeat the year. A feature of most school rooms was the **gallery**, for classes were large and the teacher needed to see all the children and all the children needed to see the teacher. These were phased out as the century progressed when individual desks and classrooms were used and when more qualified teachers were employed. The Pembrey Copperworks School was criticized in an HMI report of 1901 because "the *unsuitable galleries were not yet replaced"*. However, as the photo below of Dowlais school in 1903 indicates, the gallery was still being

Artist's impression of the gallery –Alan Williams

used in other schools. When the photo was taken the whole school was housed in one large room and the children sat in long desks in three galleries. The children in the front are exercising with dumbells under the supervision of the headteacher. It was also a way of keeping warm in the winter.

Courtesy Merthyr Libraries

Most lessons involved listening to the teacher and copying from the blackboard. There was little chance to discuss ideas and to ask questions. Along with religious education, the *3Rs* were the most important part of the curriculum. Initially, the Bible was used for reading, but they became grubby and this was regarded as disrespectful. Gradually readers or primers were published for schools which consisted of short passages from 'improving' texts, or simple paragraphs which often made little sense. They were read either around the class or a pupil was called to the front to read.

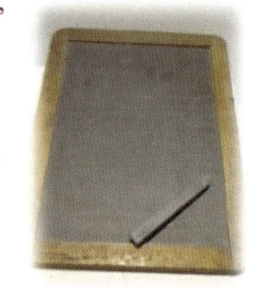

Pembrey Copperworks School

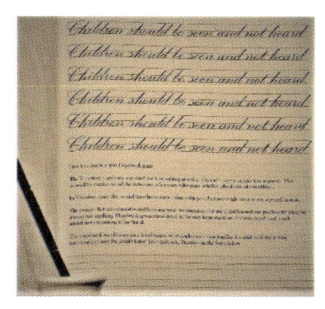

Writing meant handwriting. Paper was very expensive so many pupils wrote on slates, the scratching and squeaking of which added to an already noisy schoolroom. Infant pupils practised in sand trays while older pupils had a **copy book** into which they painfully copied moral statements from the blackboard.

One example was: "If a jobs' worth doing, it is worth doing well". A pupil later remarked: "I wrote endlessly in copy books moral maxims and poems, but I never composed a single original sentence".

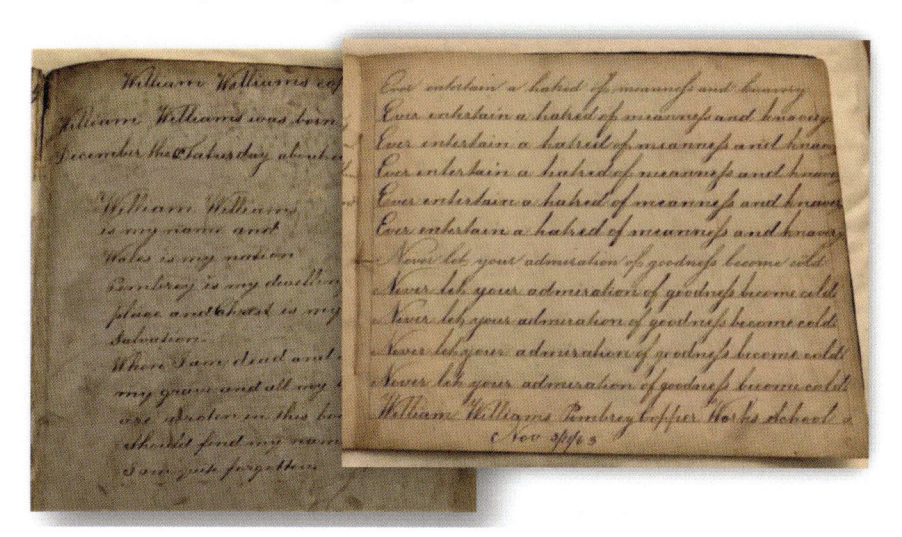

The original writing of William Williams age 11 years and a pupil at the Copperworks School in 1863. *Courtesy Nan Williams*

It was the job of the **ink monitor** to fill the inkwells each morning. When writing in their copy books in copper-plate writing children used ink pens. These didn't store ink so they had to be dipped regularly in an ink well. This often led to blots for which children were punished - hence the phrase "to blot your copy book", for which the pupil was often punished, as also was writing with

Pembrey Copperworks School

the left hand. Dictation and learning poems to recite before visitors and the school inspector was also part of the curriculum.

Each lesson normally lasted for 30 mins and there was no morning or afternoon break. In arithmetic lessons pupils were taught to add and subtract, divide and multiply. Pupils started by learning tables which would be chanted and sums were copied from the blackboard and worked out on their slates. The teacher used an **abacus** to help pupils with counting and calculations. The teacher or a pupil-teacher would walk around checking the work, which was then rubbed out ready for the next part of the lesson.

Islington Education Library

No work was saved and the pupils were expected to memorize and take in what they had been taught. Bad news for boys - they were often given harder sums to do!

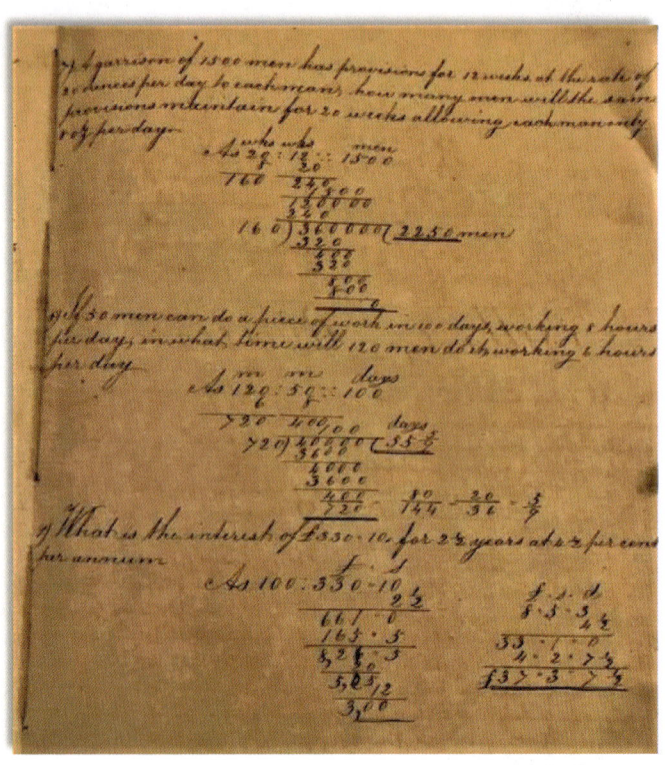

William Williams' maths at the Copperworks School 1863
Courtesy Nan Williams

The object lesson was introduced into schools to address the criticism of narrow, rote learning and to have a more child-centred approach. It was based on the teaching of Johann Heinrich Pestalozzi (1746-1827) that children learn through senses and "travel from the known to the unknown and from the concrete to the abstract".

In 1882 the Inspector commented: "In future more attention should be given to Object Lessons. Suitable apparatus for this purpose should be provided without delay". Schools could buy cabinets of objects for these lessons, which included cards with questions to help the children explore the objects. The object lesson was seen as a good vehicle for teaching science.

An object lesson *Copyright unknown*

A list of object lessons for Standard 1, taken from the School Log Book of 1886, included: *Copper, Whale, Oak Tree, Spider, Indigo, Pins, Owl, Cork, Silk, Swallow, Grape, Clock, Eagle, Timber Yard, Snail, Map of the World, Postman, Oyster, Station.*

Perhaps the school's most important event was inspection day when HMIs came to inspect virtually everything in the school. Pupils, often dressed in their best clothes, were questioned by the inspector and the children would also perform poems and songs.

Pupil teachers were also examined in all subjects and given a pass grade that enabled them to progress to the next stage of their career. For many years the awarding of a grant to the school depended on standards and attendance in the school.

The inspector would also make comments about the buildings and equipment and often made recommendations. For example: a piano was needed for the younger children. In 1893 HMI reported that the cloakroom accommodation for girls and the closet accommodation for girls and infants was insufficient and should be remedied as soon as possible. Pupils were given rewards in the form of certificates for good attendance. See the one here which is little later in 1914.

Courtesy Adrienne Thomas

The last entry in the Girls' School Log Book 1903 was: *"Wednesday 29th July, closed this school permanently at 4.30 in accordance with instructions received from Mr W.H. Cox (Clerk). Children given a treat in the shape of a tea.* **Miss E Williams, Headteacher**

Copperworks Girls' Class and headmistress Miss E. Williams. Early 1900s. *Courtesy Moira Thomas*

THE COPPERWORKS SCHOOL LOG BOOKS

Of those log books available it was possible to examine entries for the boys', girls' and infants' schools during different years. The handwriting, normally that of the headteacher, in some of the early entries was quite difficult to read and sometimes illegible. The logs of the boys' school were much fuller in content. In 1862 a new code of regulations demanded that the Principal Teacher must at least once a week enter a statement of progress, withdrawals, commencements, illness and cautions and school inspectors would inspect the log book at every visit.

Below are some of the main features of the Boys and Girls schools in the earlier years of the school:

There were **daily comments on attendance and progress**. Generally, attendance was poor. One statement in October 1878 suggested that almost half of the whole school – 229 children – had been too irregular in their attendance to be examined. The bad weather and Llanelly market were crucial factors in attendance There was also considerable absenteeism by teachers.

Registers were examined regularly. In one entry the headteacher complained that a senior teacher was very careless and forgetful and did not mark the register until 2.30.

The schools were inspected at least once a year and the headteacher would write a summary and make it available to managers and board members. The amount of the grant awarded by the company as a result of the inspection was entered at the end of the report.

The girls generally received more complimentary reports than the boys but these varied from year to year. A typical comment: "The girls are bright and clean and under fair discipline....the reading in the higher standards was very creditable...."; "the arithmetic merits special praise"; "grammar was weak especially in the higher standards". However, standards were noticed to fall at one point with a change in the teacher.

Standards in the boys' school were generally good but the school received more negative comments than the girls. For example: "greater attention should be paid to the handwriting and spelling in the higher standards"; "arithmetic of the older boys was weak". Teaching, however, was often described in very favourable terms – e.g. "vigorous and intelligent".

Speaking Welsh was frowned upon – "Welsh is so much spoken in this school that the children can scarcely comprehend what is said to them". However, there is no evidence of the use of the 'Welsh Not' and this was never Government policy.

Pupil-teachers were examined in much the same way as the children in reading, writing and arithmetic. One is spoken of in a scathing manner – "20 minutes late today"; "very careless about his duties"; "homework not half done"; "is useless as a teacher".

There were examples of dubious behaviour in the boys' school: "....the unlawful possession of two shillings.... sentenced each of the above boys to a stroke with the cane on each hand....".

After 1862 there was payment by results and grants from the Government depended partly on outcomes of examinations which were conducted by school inspectors. On one occasion the payment of a grant was threatened "unless a more favourable report is received from HMI as to attainment and general efficiency".

Teaching spaces were crowded: a teacher complained that "the class was large and I had to contend with the usual difficulty of making myself heard in a crowded room with the other classes at full work".

Copperworks Boys' Class with headmaster Mr. George P. Lewis – early 1900s
Copyright unknown

The INFANT LOG BOOK started in 1876 and here are some of the key features:

There were **health issues**. Diet, poor housing and sanitation meant that children were at this time under constant threat from the killer diseases of cholera, measles and scarlet fever. The Log Book of October 1870 and January 1871 reported the death of children from measles and scarlet fever. The dentist regularly visited the school to inspect teeth.

The Elkington family, particularly Howard and Gerard Elkington, as part founders and sponsors of the school, took a great interest in what went on there and were frequent visitors. A log entry of 16th February 1876 states that Howard Elkington looked at the children's copy books from class 1 and the children sang him a song, 'The Last Rose of Summer', which they had learnt.

An explosion had taken place in the colliery and on 3rd November 1877 the Log states that Rev. Watkins from Tabernacle Baptist Chapel came to talk about it with the children who were then given a half day holiday on account of the funerals being held that day.

There were **frequent closures and poor attendance** during bad weather - snow, extreme cold, or storms. This also included closures for very hot days. One HMI Report dated 1898 states that "a door should be fitted to stop the rain and cold blowing into the classroom occupied by the younger infants".

The children attended many of **the music and singing festivals** held in the chapels, for which they were given holidays. In 1887, for example, there were festivals at the Welsh Congregational Chapel, Tabernacle Baptist Chapel and at Jerusalem. On April 7th 1887 there was a **half day holiday** for Pembrey Fair. There were also unofficial holidays often recorded in the Log, such as market days in Llanelly when attendance was very poor and when in October 1891 help was needed for potato digging. But on July 13th 1903 the whole school was given an official half day holiday when **Buffalo Bill** came to Llanelly.

As with the Girls and Boys Schools the Infant School was **regularly inspected**. Much attention was given to discipline and a phrase quoted in the 1882 inspection - "This department is under fair discipline" - was often used and seems in today's parlance to be "satisfactory". It was also important that the children should come to school "clean and tidy" and be regular in attendance. One HMI report in 1901 tells us that the lessons were too long and that a piano was needed for the younger children. Inspectors also commented that the class was too big.

Overall, the verdict on the Copperworks Infant School was a positive one. On the whole the children were well "instructed" and the school buildings for their time were good and the school was well resourced. There were a few qualified teachers at the school and there was provision for assistant teachers and pupil-teachers to have further training.

TEACHERS IN THE 19TH CENTURY

Lord Macaulay
Wikimedia Commons

At the beginning of the 19th century **the status of the teacher** was extremely low. The well-known words of Lord Macaulay are extremely harsh but with some truth when he described the schoolmaster as: "the refuse of all other callings, discarded footmen, ruined pedlars, men who cannot work a sum in the rule of three, men who do not know whether the earth is a sphere or a cube, men who do not know whether Jerusalem is in Asia or America. And to such men, men to whom none of us would entrust the key of his cellar, we have entrusted the mind of the rising generation, and with the mind of the rising generation, the freedom, the happiness, the glory of our country."

As an occupation it was precarious and uncertain and full of largely untrained and unskilled people. Teaching was often the job of single women who normally left when they got married. When the first headteacher of the Pembrey Copperworks Boys School, Richard Williams, left to become the postmaster in Burry Port it was no doubt to a 'superior' occupation. It would not be uncommon for the teacher of a school to be in charge of a hundred children with little help and also do the job of the caretaker and handyman. Little attracted someone to teaching except to make a contribution to the education of the poor. For it was said of the teacher that his income was not much more than that of an agricultural labourer, and "very rarely equal to that of a moderately skilled mechanic".

In 'Hard Times', Charles Dickens has school board Superintendent Thomas Gradgrind berating a newly trained teacher: "Now, what I want is Facts. Teach these boys and girls nothing but Facts. Facts alone are wanted in life. Plant nothing else, and root out everything else". At this time a certificated headteacher might, with a combination of Government grant topped up by

Wikimedia Commons

the school management, earn up to around £60 plus a house. Women earned two thirds of that. Indeed, those who wanted to improve education and make it available to the ordinary working classes and the poor realised that the key was to train teachers. There were examples of teachers getting together for mutual self-improvement, but it was the introduction of the **'monitorial system'** that gave some impetus to the idea of preparing people for the job of teaching.

The Monitorial System

When the Pembrey Copperworks School was opened in 1855 the staffing included three paid monitors in the girls' school and one in the boys' school. They were at that time paid by the managers of the school. The monitorial system was developed by **Joseph Lancaster** in London and **Andrew Bell** in Madras. Lancaster, an English Quaker, established a 'training' institution in connection with his free boarding school for poor children at the Borough Road in London. Unable to pay for additional teachers, he used selected 'monitors' from the school to teach younger children who were, in large numbers, sitting in a hall in rows, and often in a gallery. The schoolmaster would teach the monitors who would relay the lesson to the row. It was formal and almost militaristic with an emphasis on rote learning and memorization.

The training at Borough Road was around three months and comprised of learning the system of which the school was regarded as a model. It was not so much education as learning the formula and tricks of the system, and the system was essentially about economy and efficiency. The regime was strict and arduous. Rising at 5.00am, the boys would spend an hour before 7.00am in private study after which they assembled in a Bible class and were questioned in their knowledge of the Scriptures. They worked as monitors in the school for three hours in the morning and three also in the afternoon. For another two hours they received instruction in subjects and the rest of the evening was spent in preparing exercises for the following day.

There were also similar schools set up by the Anglican Church and inspired by Andrew Bell, a Scottish Episcopalian priest. The competition with Lancaster's non-denominational approach was the catalyst for the establishment of 'The National Society for Promoting the Education of the Poor in the Principles of the Established Church', known as the National Society. The British and Foreign Schools Society and the National Society remained in a state of opposition and tension for many years.

Andrew Bell
Creative Commons

Pupil-Teachers

In the early years of the Pembrey Copperworks School two pupil-teachers were employed in the girls' school and two in the boys' school, all financed by the Government. The pupil-teacher system arose from the work of **David Stow (1793-1864) and James Kay-Shuttleworth (1804-1877)**, the former a Free Church Scottish pioneer in teacher training and the latter a politician and educationist. Until their influence there was little change in teacher training despite the fact that the monitorial system was recognised as deficient in that it did not educate the 'teachers' and was largely mechanistic. Neither were there secondary schools to provide a basis for training at a mature age.

Stow's method involved 'the interaction of the cultivated with the less cultivated mind' and was based on training knowledgeable teachers who were both instructed in school subjects and were taught teaching skills. There were still examples of masters and mistresses who were unable to write and, in some cases, unable to read. His Glasgow 'normal training seminary' and school, opened in 1836, was effectively the first teacher-training college in Great Britain and his trained teachers were sent out to schools throughout the country and beyond.

Kay-Shuttleworth, as one of the Assistant Poor Law Commissioners and secretary of the Committee of Council for Education between 1839 and 1849, believed that the way to improve the education of the working class was to improve the training of teachers and attract those of a good character. Influenced by David Stow's approach and impressed by the seminaries in Switzerland, he developed the idea of apprenticing selected monitors as 'pupil teachers' for a period of five years. They needed to be called to a simple life of educating poor children and would be trained in character and knowledge. His training college for teachers at Battersea, opened in 1839-40, was the first in England.

James Kay-Shuttleworth
Wikimedia Commons

In 1846 Kay-Shuttleworth launched a national scheme of pupil-teachers in which, under Government inspection, the brightest scholars would be apprenticed for five years (from 13-18 years of age) to the headmaster or headmistress providing that the teacher was competent to conduct the apprenticeship. The pupil-teachers (along with any stipendiary monitors) would be examined each year and be paid from £10 to £20 and from £5 to £12 10s. respectively, according to the length of service and gender.

The master or mistress would be paid for their training and supervision - £5 for one, or £9 for two, or £12 for three pupil teachers and £3 per annum more for each additional apprentice. When the apprenticeship was completed pupil-teachers could enter a competitive examination (the 'Queens's Scholarship') which would admit the pupil-teacher to a place in a training college with a grant of £25 for men and £20 for women.

As a result of the pressure placed upon the s a result of the pressure placed upon the headteacher to supervise the pupil-teacher **Pupil Teacher Centres** came into operation in 1881. The hours of pupil teachers were reduced and they might attend classes at a centre for part of the day.

The life of the pupil-teacher was challenging. In the earlier times the day would involve 1½ hours instruction from the master or mistress, 5 hours teaching, one hour looking after books and apparatus and also evening private study. It was a cheap way of providing staff although restrictions were later placed upon the number of children (40) for each pupil-teacher. By 1860 the training college system was flourishing and 34 colleges were providing training for 2,388 students. This was to a large extent the result of the pupil-teacher system which was turning out better teachers but the standard of teaching was still poor and they were criticised for being too mechanical, pedantic, dry and bookish in their approaches. However, the system was successful in bridging the gap between the elementary school and the training institution, and ironically delayed the introduction of what was really needed – a proper secondary educational provision.

Dowlais School Merthyr 1855 with pupil teachers.

Despite the growth in training colleges, by 1900 only 30% of elementary teachers were trained and certified. It seems around 25% were certified but untrained and 45% were former pupil-teachers who were neither trained at colleges nor certified in any other way.

WOMEN AS TEACHERS

"The hand that rocks the cradle rules the world", so says the old adage. But it gives a somewhat false impression of the status of women - their sphere was very much the hearth and home. When in 1870 all children were to be given the opportunity of a school education the girls' curriculum was very much directed towards subjects that would help them be "good wives" and home managers.

Courtesy Wikimedia Commons

In the 19th century there were not many jobs open to women outside the home, but teaching was to become one of them. There had always been governesses for the rich, ragged schools and dame schools for the poor, as well as the Sunday Schools as the great educators of what were regarded as the 'lower orders'. Yet as the school movement grew it became apparent that teachers with some kind of training were needed, and the pupil teacher, following the demise of the monitorial system, was seen as a way to address this.

Mathilde Bowser, from Pembrey Copperworks School, became a pupil-teacher in 1889. Boys and girls became pupil-teachers usually around the age of 13 to 15 years, but many boys later left the training to pursue more lucrative jobs. Although pay was not high, women were attracted to teaching because it promised reasonable pay and better prospects than factory work or domestic service. It also provided independence for unmarried women, even though they were paid less than men. For example, a male pupil-teacher was on average paid £13.9d per year while a female was paid £12.15s.

A typical profile of a girl pupil-teacher was given by a witness to the Newcastle Commission in 1861. The girl would come from a large working class family, perhaps the only older girl, and she would have to do her share of household tasks, both for the good of the family and also for her own good. For if she failed to get a Queen's Scholarship, or if she did marry, she would not be a good housewife not having had experience of domestic life. Parents might be suspicious that a certified schoolmistress "will not be the person to whom sensible and thoughtful parents of humble life will care to entrust with the formation of the character of their girls".

At the end of their pupil teacher apprenticeship the pupil teachers could take the Queen's scholarship exam and, if they passed, could go on to a training college for which grants were given, or they could remain in the classroom as unqualified teachers and continue to take exams and be annually tested by the School Inspector.

Mathilde Bowser, a Copperworks headteacher, never married. Women teachers when they married were expected to resign. This was the case until after the second world war when the marriage bars for women in teaching and the civil service began to be dissolved.

Infant staff of a Merthyr Board School 1916
Courtesy Merthyr Libraries

Women were also held to a high moral code. They were expected to conform to and to demonstrate the values and attitudes of the Christian faith, often to a greater extent than their male colleagues. Also, a certain dress code was expected and some education committees forbade the wearing of "flowers, ornaments or finery", since they were afraid it might distract their pupils. A sober style of dress was required.

Victorian society was dominated by social class, and this proved to be the case for teachers as well. Dorothea Beale, one of the promotors of higher education for women, stated in 1866 that her school admitted only the daughters of independent or professional men. While at the other end of the spectrum Elizabeth Andrews records how she had a great desire to be a teacher and how, as an unpaid helper in the classroom supported by her headmistress, she was unable to start as a pupil-teacher. The family couldn't afford the extra train fare to Aberdare College even though she would have been paid as a pupil teacher. More importantly she was needed to help out at home and her career was very much secondary.

It was thought that working class parents would not want their daughters to be taught by middle class teachers who would give them ideas above their station, so it was not seen as important for women to train to a higher level and for them to go to training college or university They would continue in the classroom learning "on the job", being paid less and an attractive employment opportunity for Education Boards.

To become a pupil-teacher a certain level of education was required. As well as good standards in reading, grammar, arithmetic and geography, girls also were expected be able to sew neatly and to knit. When training as a pupil-teacher expectations were not as high for girls as they were for boys, and the curriculum presented to them not so rigorous. For example, algebra, surveying, use of the globes and geography of the British Empire was substituted by special proficiency in sewing.

The scale of payments to schoolmistresses was two-thirds of that of men, which diminished their status even though gradually women proved themselves academically to be the equal of men in education. 'Domestic economy' was always an extra for women for the ties of women to hearth and home proved difficult to break.

There is no doubt that the mass education of the poor eventually allowed women a way in to a professional career in education but, as in all areas of life, it was a long hard struggle to gain some kind of equality with men.

MATHILDE BOWSER
Pupil-teacher and Headteacher

Courtesy Gaynor Mills

In October 1918 Miss Mathilde Bowser returned to the Copperworks School in Burry Port as Headmistress. She had been a pupil there and later it was here that she began her teaching career as a pupil-teacher. Born in 1874 she was the eldest child of Captain George Bowser (1829-1911), grandson of the industrialist who had come to Burry Port in 1787 to mine coal and eventually help develop the two harbours.

Mathilde was born in France, hence the different spelling of her name. Her father, Captain Bowser, needed to put into the port of Dunkirk, where his wife Ann gave birth to a daughter, Mathilde. The family lived first in Cardiff and then moved to Burry Port. The 1881 census shows her living with her three siblings, Ann, Robert and George, at the Harbour View Hotel at the dock side where her father was the licensee.

Mathilde was a pupil at the Copperworks School, and, while still a child there, she decided that she wanted to be a teacher. In 1889, aged 15, she signed a memorandum of agreement, which was similar to an apprentice indenture. She would start a four year term of service at the school. Her salary was £8 a year with an annual increment if she passed the necessary examinations and fulfilled various other conditions.

A large part of her training was under the supervision of the headmistress, Miss E. Williams. She would have had a strict regime to follow, as laid

Miss E. Williams

down in her memorandum of agreement. A certain amount of time would be spent teaching groups of children under the direction of the headmistress, for which she would have to prepare. Her professional education would include lessons on grammar, writing essays on English history or poetry, map work as well as mathematical subjects.

Mathilde would have been examined in these and other subjects by the School Inspector and the results recorded in the log book. We read about her as a first year pupil-teacher: *"E. Edmunds and M. Bowser have passed fairly, but M. Bowser should attend to Composition, Needlework and Writing"*. She is mentioned in the log books of 1891 as a 2nd year pupil teacher who passed fairly but needed to attend to Geography, History and Method.

Mathilde Bowser next went as a pupil-teacher to Pentre Board School in the Rhondda, from where she left for Cardiff in 1898 and taught at Grangetown Board School where she is mentioned in the South Wales Daily News as one of a list candidates being examined in First Year Papers. In 1911 Mathilde was still teaching in Cardiff, boarding with a family in Canton and now described as an assistant teacher. From Cardiff she returned to Burry Port to become headmistress of Pinged School and moved into a bungalow next to her old home, Harbour View. It was here she would live for the rest of her life.

Courtesy Ray Hobbs

From Pinged school in 1918 Mathilde Bowser came full circle and was appointed headmistress of the **Copperworks Infants' School** and stayed in that post as headmistress until she retired in 1934. The school was warmly known as "The Bowser School" by her ex- pupils and the local people well after she had retired. As an old lady she was affectionately known around the town as "Tilly Bowser", always busy and 'up and doing'.

The indomitable Miss Bowser lived alone in her bungalow by the harbour, fiercely independent. In retirement she travelled widely through Europe and in 1940, then in her late seventies, spent some time in the USA in Allen, Indiana. Perhaps she had inherited the spirit of adventure from her sea captain father. While there she developed a deep dislike of television - she decided it was "not to her taste" and when she returned home refused to have one in her house. "Television! I just could not sit and look at it; I want to be up and doing". Mathilde Bowser died in Bryntirion Hospital, Llanelli in 1971 aged 98.

Mathilde Bowser had one regret in her life, that she had never visited Russia, a country which had fascinated her after seeing the film 'Leningrad' many years earlier. "But I couldn't find anyone to go with me. I think that perhaps I may have left it too late to go now."

Children of the school in the mid-1920s when Mathilde was headmistress. *Courtesy Caroline*

THE 'TREASON OF THE BLUE BOOKS'

In 1844 in South Wales 45% of married men and 70% of married women were unable to write their own names, according to a government report. This is one indication of the poor state of education in the country at this time. In the same year the commissioners of the enquiry into the Rebecca Riots had suggested that the disturbances were partly due to the lack of educational facilities and in particular to the ignorance of the English language which they saw as a serious impediment to any general improvement. Lack of spoken English was regarded as a serious handicap to workers' involvement in society, career advancement or change of occupation.

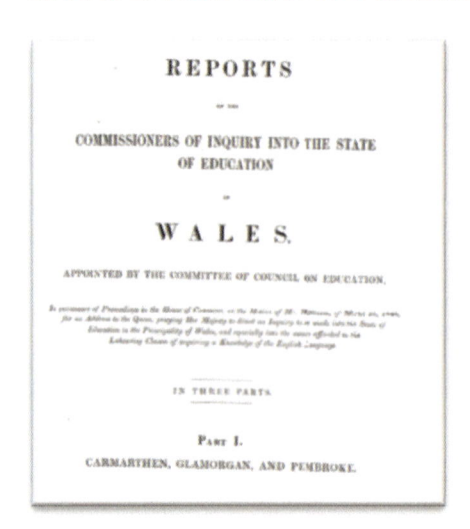

Many people in Wales would have agreed that they needed English to get on in the wider world and Rev. David Rees of Llanelli, editor of *Y Diwygiwr,* reflected this view when he wrote that "we should be ready to welcome the spread of English…however much we may regret the passing of the sonorous and adequate old Welsh language…". It was a Welshman, William Williams, born in Carmarthenshire who raised the issue of education in Wales in the House of Commons in 1846 and argued that the government should set up a state system of elementary education in Wales following an enquiry into the state of education in Wales. 'Law and order' could be improved by education.

William Williams MP
Wikimedia Commons

It was James Kay-Shuttlesworth who appointed the three commissioners for the enquiry and gave them their instructions. None of the three had any educational experience or knowledge of the Welsh language, and they appointed assistants to help them. In Carmarthenshire the Commissioner, **Ralph Lingen**, a classical scholar and barrister, was assisted by a nonconformist from Merthyr and two Anglican students from Lampeter.

Ralph Lingen MP
Wikimedia Commons

The instructions to the commissioners included identifying the existing number of schools for the education of the children of the labouring classes or adults, attendance, the ages of the scholars, the character of the instruction, condition of the school, the language of instruction etc. But the offence to the people of Wales was mainly caused by the requirement to report on the character of the people and how an improved education system might be influential on "the general condition of society and its moral and religious progress".

The report is hundreds of pages long, a tedious and repetitive read at times but an invaluable glimpse into society at the time. It is scathing in its attack on the state of education in Wales; the tone was often derisory and the approach lacking in empathy. It portrayed an insufficient number of schools, inadequately trained teachers and too few children attending school and with irregular attendance. The reason for the latter was often the inability to pay the school pence and family responsibilities. The teaching of English, the medium of instruction in most schools, was poor. Most children had no knowledge of English and often neither did the teachers. Others used English text books which the children could not read.

The commissioners did praise a number of features:

The Sunday schools enabled people to gather as equals, providing worship, some discussion and instruction and in which some displayed leadership skills. Although regarded as "real fields of mental activity" they were seen as limited largely to reading the scriptures in a repetitive way and moral and religious instruction. They were never a substitute for the day school, although they were

19th century Sunday School, with permission from Victorianweb.org.

recognised as the major force for literacy in the Welsh language. Often the behaviour of the children was disruptive. The church Sunday schools (as opposed to the chapel), however, were quite different, often led by clergy and with more competent teachers.

Accommodation for schools was generally poor but there were a few good ones of "a scholastic appearance". For example, in the parish of Llanybydder Colonel Wood's school had a triple tier of benches one side, desks the other, a teacher's desk and fireplace. Although the room had walls of rough-hewn stone there was nothing of the "untidiness and squalor" often described. Arithmetic, spelling and geography was taught from a large slate and there were maps and coloured prints on the wall.

The learning ability of the Welsh people was often commended (what they called "the native intelligence") in that they were able "to learn well that which was taught badly". With regard to the Bible, their reading and skill in discussing it theologically was superior to their English counterparts. Yet mental activity was restricted largely to theological ideas.

The Commissioners criticised a range of aspects of education and behaviour:

- **The Welsh language** was identified early in the report as an issue: *"My district exhibits the phenomenon of a peculiar language isolating the mass from the upper portion of society"*. It was described as *"a language of the old-fashioned agriculture, of theology, and of simple rustic life"* which stopped a Welsh man from getting to the top of the social scale ("keeps him under the hatches") or entering the office since he lacked the ability to communicate in a world of English and is isolated within his narrow sphere of activity from other influences. Yet they recognised that parents wanted their children to learn English although Welsh was the language of their life.

Courtesy Wikimedia Commons

- **Among the agricultural and manufacturing quarters** there was little evidence of a sound education. Most farmers could write little more than their names, were not much better educated than their labourers and struggled to keep efficiently their accounts.

- **The number of buildings** used for schools In Carmarthenshire which were in bad repair was around 36%. To give an example, one school was held in a part of the dwelling house and scholars reached it by means of a ladder through a hole in the loft. The room was lit by one small glazed window half of which was patched up with boards. The furniture consisted of one table, and a few broken benches. There were several large holes in the floor and the room was dark. Indeed, just over 10% of school buildings were legally secured for educational purposes and a school might be in the teacher's home, the kitchen of a farmhouse, an adjacent outbuilding, a loft, the church or chapel itself.

- **The average age of teachers** was 40 years and only about 12% were trained. They came from a wide variety of previous occupations including school assistants, commercial clerks, carpenters, milliners, domestic servants, farmers, mariners, married women, ministers. They were held in low esteem. In one school it was recorded that *"the schoolmaster unites with his educational duties the somewhat anomalous functions of barber and layer out of the dead"*. There was a large number of 'private adventure' schools, mostly of extremely poor standard, since anyone could open a school irrespective of experience.

- One of the problems identified in country schools was the **lack of uniformity of books** and also of apparatus. Bibles provided some consistency but each child would bring to school a different book for learning to read. This was not the case in the works schools. In some schools extra payment was required for the teaching of writing and arithmetic and most of the time other subjects such as history and geography would not be available.

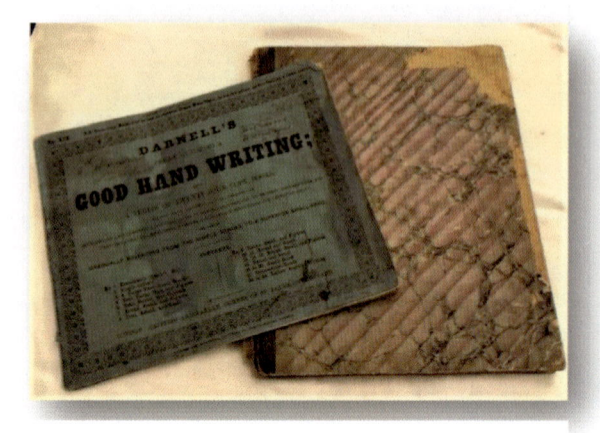

Courtesy Nan Williams

- **Ventilation** was a problem and inspectors complained about hot sickening smells in rooms with up to 50 children huddled together. They described *"squalid and miserable hovels"* and it was not uncommon for children to kneel on a floor of bare earth writing on an old door laid upon on benches. Conversely, some schools were cold, drafty and with thatched, leaking roofs. The majority of places used for a school had no toilet facilities.

- **Poverty** was the main reason preventing the labouring classes from attending school. Wages were low and it was a struggle for parents to provide a good diet. Not only was attendance irregular and neither was it accurately recorded. Difficulty in communicating by road in the winter was an issue, but the commissioners also noted the holding of an undue number of fairs takes place "*at which drinking is practised no less than buying and selling*". In one village of 1700 people there were 47 public houses and nine fairs held in the course of the year. Poverty was also the reason for the observation that "*in their habits the labouring classes are particularly dirty*" with animals allowed in the houses and lack of toilets.

- It was in fact the comments in the Blue Books on **the people's behaviour** that caused the most offence. There were claims of 'immorality' between the sexes, chiefly among farm servants who had to share accommodation at night. Unmarried servants were known to "*range the country at night*" and were admitted into houses by the servants or met up at the public houses. Even the nightly prayer meetings at the chapels were claimed to be places where lovers met up and the "*Welsh peasant girl is almost universally unchaste*".

- **Men were criticised** for indecency in washing naked before the women and women for changing their undergarments before the men. Both were criticised for sleeping in the same room, whether married or single. Those comments referring to Llanelly and Pembrey paint an improved picture with drunkenness the main problem.

Ironically, the observations provided for the commissioners by Llanelly industrialists Richard Nevill and William Chambers Junior are the most devastating. They complained of the Llanelly people's "*disregard of truth and the laxity of morals*", a lack of parental responsibility and wives are "*mostly slovenly and improvident, and as mothers ignorant and injudicious*".

PEMBREY SCHOOLS

There are three Pembrey day schools mentioned in the report, visited on February 10th and 11th 1847 by the inspecting assistant William Brown. The Sunday Schools are listed with the information in columns.

1. **Trim Saron, 1843**. This was a National School (i.e. linked to the Anglican National Society) but supported mainly by the iron masters Messrs. Norton, Upperton and Stone who paid four shillings a week to the mistress for teaching their workmen's children. The children were required also to pay 1d per week, but it seems not all managed to do that. Farmers' children paid 2d a week. The mistress was said to speak English *"tolerably well"*. The furniture consisted of one table, one desk, and four benches. Some of the copy books were *"tolerably well written"*. Plans were mentioned of a new school to replace the small building for 40 pupils and Norton and Stone had pledged £100 towards it.

Stanley's School
Courtesy family of John Nicholson

2. **Furnace school, 1845**. A private adventure school, it is more often referred to as **'Stanley's School'** after the mine owner, John Stanley and met in the upper storey of an iron works building. The report states that the master was a clergyman's son and had received a good education. The scholars were the children of farmers and labourers, but on the day visited there were very few children present because of the snow. *"The copy books were kept very clean and were well written"*.

3. **Richard Hall's school, 1834**. A private adventure school, the master of the school is described as "an illiterate man" and the scholars were principally labourers' children.

Nine Sunday Schools are listed and those with the highest number of children attending were Rehoboth, Pembrey (110), Bethel, Pembrey (97),

Pwll Baptist (92) and Jerusalem, Burry Port (76). The others listed were Ebenezer (Hermon); the Church Vestry Room Pembrey; Gwscwm (Tabernacle); Pencaerdrysi Pinged; Sardis Trimsaron. In most of them the teaching was in both English and Welsh and generally at least a third of the pupils were described as being able to read. Bibles and 'elementary books' were used for reading.

The report came to be known as the 'Treason of the Blue Books' from the colour of its cover, and because it caused a furore especially with regard to derogatory comments made about the behaviour and morals of the Welsh people.

Although they worked incredibly hard, covered a huge number of day and Sunday schools and the information they provided is very detailed, the commissioners and their assistants have been regarded as unqualified for the job. Their background and upbringing did not give them any understanding of the communities they were investigating.

Another point of criticism was that four out of five of the inspectors were Churchmen in a country that was primarily nonconformist. The commissioners were regarded as having overemphasised and exaggerated a dark side to Welsh life and it was claimed that it was often a case of Anglican clergyman painting an unfavourable picture of the activities among the Nonconformists, whom they regarded as their opposition.

It was pointed out that the team had no experience of examining schools nor any conception of what could be reasonably taught in an elementary school. Furthermore, the approach was inappropriate and the questions asked were misleading. For example, 'Peter was one of the prophets, was he not?'

In truth, the educational situation was extremely poor, but no poorer than many areas in England. The commissioners in fact recognised the hunger that the Welsh had for education and especially praised the work of the Sunday Schools. What the grim report did was to dramatically raise awareness of the dire state of education in Wales and the inadequacy of the teaching and stir into action the Societies responsible for the provision of education. But at the same time it hardened attitudes toward Anglicanism and increased the competition between the two societies supporting Anglicanism and Nonconformism. The need was recognised for the intervention of the state but this came slowly and by the time of the 1870 Education Act government grants to school provided for only 60% of the pupil places needed.

SIR JOSIAH MASON – Businessman, Educational Benefactor and Philanthropist

The early days

Josiah Mason was very much a self-made man. He had no formal training, had no trade and served no apprenticeship. Yet he is admired for his natural resolution, ingenuity, industry and by an innate conviction that he must do something in the world, both for himself and for others.

Courtesy Josiah Mason Trust

His father was a carpet weaver in Kidderminster and his parents were unable to give him anything beyond the merest elements of school teaching. The education he did have was at a Dame school held in a cottage next door to his father's house. From the age of eight years he began to work in some sort of business. At first it was selling cakes in the streets - Jo's cakes - to a regular clientele. At one time he collected copper money and wrapped them up in five-shilling packets, and was remunerated by the fee of one penny for every pound. His last street trading was in fruit and vegetables which he sold door-to-door.

At the age of 15 he was shoemaking, an occupation he could do at home while looking after his elder brother who was unable to work. During this time he taught himself to write and even obtained some casual work as a letter writer for poor people. He read a wide range of books - theology, history and science - and in his studies was helped by lessons at the Unitarian Sunday school and later at the Wesleyan Sunday school. He was involved in a number of jobs including shop keeping, carpentry, house painting and back to carpet weaving.

However, wages were low in Kidderminster and opportunities were few. It was the move from Kidderminster to Birmingham that opened up for him the most promising employment, the first with his uncle at his glass works until a disagreement with his uncle. As a result of a growing reputation for energy, enthusiasm and business knowledge, he was appointed as a manager of a business making split rings. This business he eventually bought and developed, making it extremely profitable by his industry and ingenuity in introducing a stamping which made the ring at a single blow.

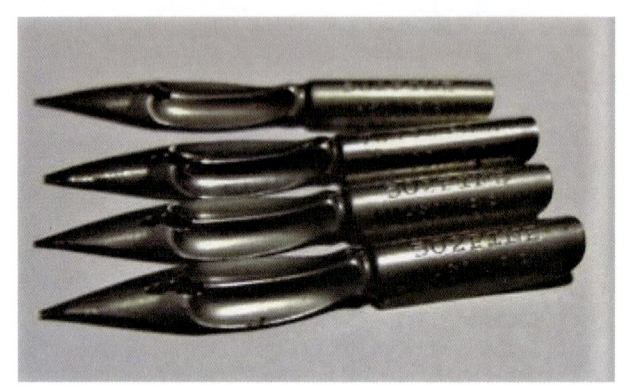

It was here that he introduced the lucrative steel pen trade. Then, in 1829 he spotted in a shop window some pens made by James Perry of London.

Original nibs made in Mason's factory and with both Mason's and Perry's names on them. *Copyright Authors*.

Convinced he could do better, Mason bought one of the pens, took it home and overnight produced three pens which he sent to James Perry. He liked them and, for the next 46 years Josiah Mason made every Perry pen and became the world's largest pen maker, although he sold very few pens in his own name. He was now only 28 years old and, as a result of his passion for improvement, was employing almost 1000 people. The difference he brought to the process of making pens was to include the slitting by machine enabling them to be sold cheaply as articles of common use. Mason himself had made the punches required for the slitting and the processes were kept secret.

Elkington and Mason

In the 1840s George and Henry Elkington, in their Birmingham factory, were working on applying the electro-plating process in a commercial way. Up to about 1840 the method of plating used in Birmingham and Sheffield was that of hand plating of silver on copper which was slow and costly. Research by a number of scientists which involved immersion in various solutions resulted in an electro-plating process which had commercial possibilities. After the research of John Wright which stabilised the process, the Elkingtons needed finance and organisation to ensure the progress and development of the industry.

The front of the former Elkington and Mason factory today

In 1842 Josiah Mason entered into partnership with them, against the advice of many, and provided not only capital but also the required business experience and vigour. It was a risk for both Mason and Elkington since the process was new and relatively untried and doubts were expressed about the durability of the articles to be produced. The Elkington Archive suggests that George Elkington put £55,000 pounds into the business, Mason put £35,000 and the profits were one third to Mason and two thirds to Elkington.

If successful it would displace the slow and costly system of hand plating but it would take all of Mason's organising ability and business capacity for it to succeed. Mason provided suitable buildings in Newhall Street, Birmingham, and laid out the plans of the workshops according to his own arrangements. Although there was potential for ornamental articles the business also produced items for common use and to be sold at a reasonable price - for example, spoons and forks.

The partnership, dating from 1842, lasted until 1865 and was dissolved just before the death of George Elkington. On a number of occasions he had been invited by Herr Alfred Krupp, the director of the famous steel works at Essen, to become part of his establishment. However, Mason declined, preferring to stay in employment in Birmingham.

The Copper Works

The firm's ingenious chemist, Alexander Parkes, developed a process for smelting copper ore and purifying the copper by means of phosphorous. Elkington and Mason acquired the patent and they needed a copper works for the smelting at a place which was convenient to receive the copper ore, mainly at first from Cornwall. Parkes had suggested a site near Llanelly and Elkington and Mason, after visiting South Wales, favoured an area 3 miles away

Elkington and Mason sauce ladle plated on Burry Port smelted copper – *Copyright Authors*

where there was already a dock available. Although Swansea was the centre of copper smelting at the time, Mason was keen to move along the coast from the pollution and build where the air was fresher. What later became Burry Port was described by one early publication as "nothing to be seen but the neglected dock, one public house and an extensive tract of sand – a rabbit warren". The same publication sums up: "Excellent works were laid out with great rapidity, large, well-built, and specially designed to secure the health of the men engaged in them….. The proprietors of the new Pembrey Copper Works were disposed specially to take care of their men…. suitable cottages were built, each cottage having a garden allotted to it; collieries were opened to supply coal; schools were erected for 350 children, and provision was made for religious instruction. In short, on the site which a little while before was a lonely and desolate rabbit warren, there grew up a thriving populace and healthy village, with the copper works as it centre, and an important trade was created, which remains in a flourishing condition to the present date" (1882).

The Copperworks School

While he was involved with the Copper Works (although, like Elkington, he never lived in Burry Port) Josiah Mason furthered his interest in the education of children. One of his great works of charity was to build the Copperworks school, now housed in two buildings on Morlan Terrace, Burry Port. Using bricks from the brickworks the company had built, Mason constructed the Copperworks School at a cost of £1,700, mainly for the children of the workers.

Initially it comprised separate boys, girls and Infant sections with about 500 pupils. It was a non-denominational school, whereas others in the area were church schools. At first, some parents were suspicious of his motives, so those who were reluctant to send their children to his school he encouraged with gifts of hats, shoes and clothes. That did the trick, although they were later charged a penny a week.

Josiah Mason - Philanthropist

Mason's great business acumen along with his energy and enthusiasm brought him great wealth. From a young boy to an old man he worked steadily and vigorously and although he had great pleasure in making money, he was not a selfish man.

His biographer in 1882 wrote: "The wealth he acquired was valued by him chiefly as the means of doing good on a great scale; he looked upon himself not so much as the owner as the steward of it.' Not only was he a benefactor in education but he had a great concern for aged and infirm people and for orphaned children and consequently his first charitable venture was an almshouse for spinsters and widows over 50 years of age and orphaned girls which opened in Erdington, a suburb of Birmingham, in 1858.

Pembrey Copperworks School

His second venture in 1868 was an almshouse and orphanage for 26 women and 300 children on a 13acre site with playgrounds and gardens.

First alms houses and orphanage, Erdington, 1858. *Courtesy Josiah Mason Trust*

His third great project was the establishment of a science college which challenged the traditional non-vocational university tradition and aimed at providing a more practical scientific education for all which linked with the artistic, manufacturing and industrial pursuits of the area.

The Josiah Mason Trust

Mason's work continues in Birmingham today in the JOSIAH MASON TRUST. It aims to provide safe, secure, affordable and well-maintained sheltered accommodation, residential care and extra care housing for adults in their older age and education and support to young people from disadvantaged communities.

Science College, 1880, now part of the University in Birmingham. *Courtesy Josiah Mason Trust*

A BRIEF OVERVIEW OF EARLY INDUSTRIAL HISTORY IN THE PEMBEY AND LLANELLI AREA

The old saying 'It takes two to tango' can well be applied to the development of industry in Llanelli and district. On the one hand one needs the industrialist, the entrepreneur, the financier; on the other hand, one needs the worker. How equitable the relationship should be has been the subject of much political debate and industrial action. Here we look briefly at some of the prominent industrialists who came in to the area of Llanelli and Burry Port before and at the time of the Copperworks School.

One day in the year 1796 a coach and wagon brought **Alexander Raby** and his family across the Falcon Bridge into Llanelli. A wealthy ironmaster, he sold his estate in England and brought the money he made to increase his fortune in Llanelli. Raby took over a furnace in the area that is now also called Furnace, added a second and used them day and night to produce 'pig iron'. Raby's furnace was heated with coal in the form of coke, and he mined his own coal from under the Stradey Estate. Having first used mules and oxen, he built a tram road which connected his furnace with his forge at Sandy and his collieries and this led down to a shipping place at Seaside, known as Squire Raby's Dock and later as the Carmarthenshire Dock. Raby was popular and paid his workers well - they were said to 'eat pound notes on well buttered sandwiches'.

Alexander Raby
Courtesy Llanelli Library

Charles Nevill, a Worcestershire copper works owner established his works in Seaside in 1805, which was further developed by his son Richard Janion Nevill. The conditions were favourable, there was coal to be mined and a new dock was built a year later to import the copper ore. The Nevills improved

Richard Janion Nevill
Llanelli Library

the flood defences and made safer the approaches with buoys to mark the channels and pilot skiffs to bring in vessels safely. Whereas their first dock was tidal, in the early 1820s the new Nevill's Dock was probably the first 'floating dock' with sluice gates to allow ships to be loaded or unloaded at any time.

The early industrialists in the Llanelli area were predominantly men, but Mary Glascott along with her sons, George and Thomas Glascott, were the proprietors of the Cambrian Copper Works in Llanelli, established in 1830 by the English Copper Company. They are described as Copper Merchants and Brass and Copper Manufacturers from Whitechapel in London. It was not a successful venture and the Works were taken over by Nevill and Co. in 1847 and used for the smelting of lead and silver. When in 1898 it was bought by the Welsh Tinplate & Metal Stamping Co. Ltd., it produced among other things enamelled saucepans and its fame led to Llanelli being nick-named 'Sospan'.

The outstanding pioneer of early industrialization in the Pembrey and Burry Port area was **George Bowser**. He moved from Middlesex to the area in the 1790s as part of the 'black gold rush' and opened a number of collieries. From his pits at Cwm Capel he first carted the coal along a rutted tramway to a shipping point at Barnaby Pill, east of Burry Port but by 1816 had laid a new tramway to Carreg Edwig, near the site of the old Pembrey Harbour. His vision was a harbour, canal and tramways in Pembrey and he went into partnership with others in the venture. The harbour opened in 1819 but Bowser withdrew and later backed the development of a new harbour in Burry Port and a new tramroad from Cwm Capel.

From fields, marshes and dunes the landscape of Burry Port was now changing and even more so with the horse-drawn tramroad converted to a standard gauge railway to take steam locomotives. This was the product of the new copper works owners, **George Elkington and Josiah Mason**, whose copper works was constructed in 1849 to supply copper to their electroplating factory in Birmingham and for general sale. The site alongside the harbour enabled ships to unload the copper ore which came from copper mines in Cornwall and increasingly from countries such as

Australia, Cuba and Chile. To minimise the harm from poisonous fumes the "Stac Fawr" was begun in 1850, a massive chimney of over a million bricks and 82 metres tall. The Copper Works employed large numbers in the works and even more in the company's wider interests in the area, attracted other industries to the town, but it also benefitted from existing ones like coal mining, with the works' management owning numerous mines in the vicinity.

THE WORKERS

The workers were the people who made the industrialists' vision possible.

In the first coal mines men would dig out the coal from the surface on higher ground so that the water could drain away. The coal would then be taken to a nearby shipping point on carts and later tramways, canals and railways. However, the industrial revolution demanded large quantities and with the invention of the steam engine water could be pumped out and deeper pits sunk. Alexander Raby's new pits depended on a pumping engine. Yet as mining became more expansive so did the dangers for the miners underground. Symons describes the laxity in the reporting and reluctance to acknowledge the growing number of accidents resulting in injury and death, mostly as a consequence of neglect, apathy, lack of investment and poor management by the owners. The reported causes of deaths in the coal industry in Llanelli in the middle years of the 19th century were mainly from falls of stone, coal or earth in the workings, accidents at the top and bottom of mine shafts and explosions of methane (firedamp). Children, some as young as five, were used in Llanelli's collieries for opening and closing the air doors and drawing the 'corves' by straps around their shoulders and waist. It was desperate poverty that made it necessary for families to allow their children down the mines, and, although the 1842

Drawing by Alan Williams

Mines and Collieries Act banned all girls and women and boys under 10 from working underground, this continued until the 1870s.

Alexander Raby was popular and he was said to pay his workers well. But when iron master Robert Crawshay had the words *'God Forgive Me'* carved on his tombstone it was undoubtedly to do with remorse for the misery of a hell on earth his family had brought to generations of iron workers in Merthyr. What a writer in 1884 described as "great towers of brick work, filled with burning coal or coke, melting limestone and fluid iron … perpetually vomiting flame and Stygian smoke..." did not do much for the health of the workers employed by the iron masters. They lived in luxury while workers often lived in poverty with poor water supply and inadequate sanitation. Children and young people were employed in the works filling the barrows with iron for the forge, breaking up limestone, filling up the boxes with coke at the furnace, cutting up scrap iron for the furnace and taking the cinders from the furnace.

Remains of Raby's Furnace, Llanelli
Copyright Authors

The Rollerman - *Courtesy Tata Steel*

The tinplate workers in Llanelli and Burry Port worked in very harsh conditions. One writer described the hot of the end of the works: "The heat was infernal, the fumes insufferable, the noise stupefying. Screaming-hot jagged edged plates, arcing through the air on long tongs or skidding along the iron-surfaced floor, caused burns and crippling lacerations." People worked in dangerous conditions in temperatures up to 38°C and men would drink up to 40 pints of liquid during an eight hour shift. Workers provided their own protective clothing or face horrific injuries. Tinplate might employ whole families at various stages of their lives and young people as young as 13 years. Heavy working in poorly ventilated spaces and the primitive sanitation facilities led to workers facing a future of respiratory diseases, rheumatism and other diseases and the average age at death was 45 years.

The copper works owners in Llanelli and Burry Port generally looked after their workers, providing housing and education and copper working was often regarded as the 'aristocracy of labour' with comparatively good pay and largely cordial owner-worker relationships. Yet the work was hard and often dangerous and workers might work a 24 hour shift. Noxious fumes were a constant irritant and chronic bronchitis and asthma a common consequence. The furnace man was exposed to the heat of both molten metal and the stream of slag and sometimes spills and splashes caused terrible scalding. Children as young as eight were known to be used and these might work from 6 am to 8 pm. Women and girls broke ore into small lumps and wheeled coal and ore to the furnaces. Boys cleaned ash-pits and greased machinery, wheeled coal and ore to the furnace and took ashes from it, and broke up the slag to find copper for re-melting.

Unsurprisingly from what we have described, industrialisation was accompanied by social unrest and rebellion. In Wales the most discussed examples tend to be the Chartists, Rebecca Riots and Merthyr Riots. But that is another story.

BIBLIOGRAPHY AND SOURCES

- *A History of Education in Wales*, Jones and Roderick, University of Wales Press, 2003.
- Archives of the British and Foreign Schools Society.
- *A Woman's Work Is Never Done*, Elizabeth Andrews, Honno Classics, 2006.
- *Aspects of their History, Book 1,* John A Nicholson, 1993.
- *Chapels in the Valley,* D. Ben Rees, Ffynnon Press, 1975.
- *Coal Mining in the Llanelli Area, Volume1,* M.V. Symons, Llanelli Borough Council, 1979.
- *Coal Mining in the Llanelli Area, Volume2,* M.V. Symons, Carmarthenshire CCC, 2012.
- *'Copper-Works Schools in South Wales during the Nineteenth Century',* Leslie Wynne Evans, National Library of Wales Journal, 1959, Summer Volume XI/1.
- *Copperopolis,* Stephen Hughes, 2000.
- *Copperworks School Log Books,* Carmarthenshire Archives.
- *Culture and the Nonconformist Tradition,* Ed. Shaw and Kreider, University of Wales Press, 1999.
- *Education in Industrial Wales*, Leslie Wynn Evans, Avalon Books, 1971.
- *Hafod Copperworks School,* Hafod History Society, 2002 (First published 1905)
- *History of Elementary Education in England and Wales from 1800 to the Present Day*, C. Birchenough, W.B. Clive, 1914.
- *Josiah Mason: A Biography,* John Thackray Bunce, General Books, Memphis, 1882.
- *Josiah Mason 1795-1881,* Brian Jones, Brewin Books, Studley, 1985.
- *Life in a Victorian School*, Pamela Horn, Pitkin, 2013.
- *Looking Around Llanelli*, Harry Davies, Llanelli Town Council, 1985.
- *Nonconformity in the Nineteenth Century,* David M Thompson, Routlege & Kegan Paul, 1972.
- *The Blue Books of 1847,* National Library of Wales.
- *The Victorian Schoolroom*, Trevor May, Shire Publications Ltd. 1994.
- *The Training of Teachers in England and Wales during the 19th Century*, R.W. Rich, CUP, 1933.
- 'The Welshman', 17th August, 1855.
- *The Elkington Archive,* The Library of Birmingham
- *Valley Lives, Book 1,* Merthyr Tydfil Public Libraries, 1992.
- 'Y Diwygiwr', September 1855.

Printed in Great Britain
by Amazon